Contents

Glossary

On page 24 there is a glossary of
words and terms. The glossary words
appear in **bold** in the text.

Who were knights?

Knights were tough, brave FIGHTING MEN, who lived in the **middle ages** or medieval times – from around AD 500 to AD 1500. They promised to fight loyally for kings and **lords**. In return, they were given land, treasure and castles.

It took years to train to become a knight. At eight years old, boys went to live with a knight's family. They worked as **pages**.

At 14, they began work as **squires** (helpers). They learned how to fight, looked after the knight's horses and helped him get ready for battle.

TIME TRAVELLERS

KNIGHTS
AND CASTLES

by Fiona Macdonald
Consultant Richard Tames

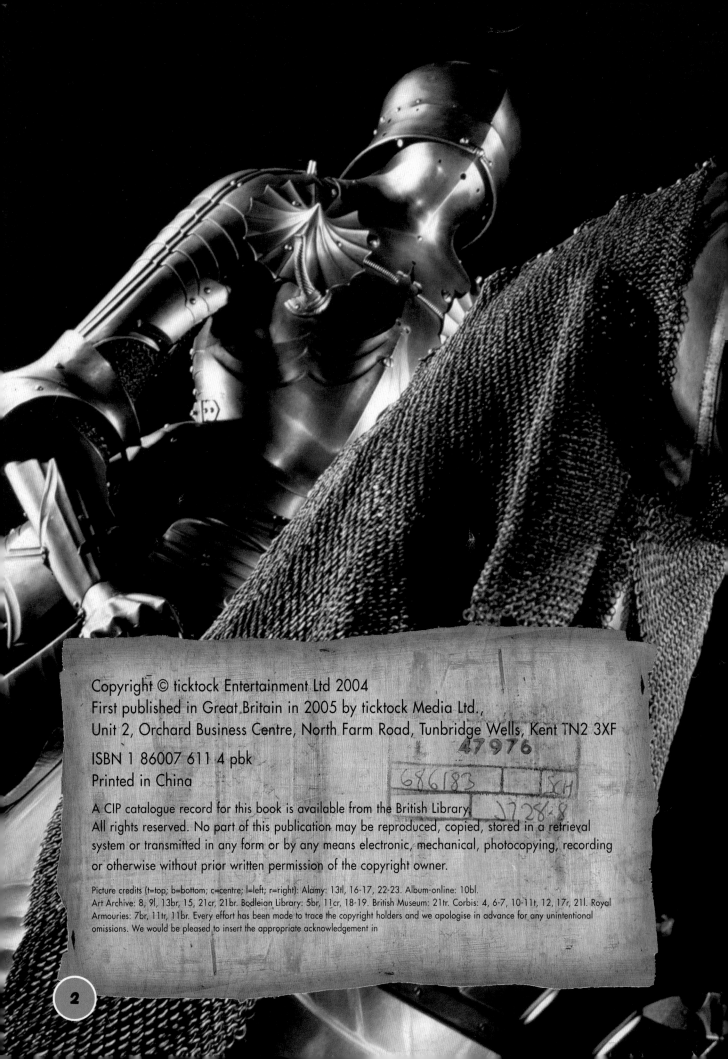

Copyright © ticktock Entertainment Ltd 2004
First published in Great Britain in 2005 by ticktock Media Ltd.,
Unit 2, Orchard Business Centre, North Farm Road, Tunbridge Wells, Kent TN2 3XF

ISBN 1 86007 611 4 pbk
Printed in China

Picture credits (t=top; b=bottom; c=centre; l=left; r=right): Alamy: 13tl, 16-17, 22-23. Album-online: 10bl.
Art Archive: 8, 9l, 13br, 15, 21cr, 21br. Bodleian Library: 5br, 11cr, 18-19. British Museum: 21tr. Corbis: 4, 6-7, 10-11t, 12, 17r, 21l. Royal
Armouries: 7br, 11tr, 11br. Every effort has been made to trace the copyright holders and we apologise in advance for any unintentional
omissions. We would be pleased to insert the appropriate acknowledgement in

At 21, squires became knights, in a special ceremony called **dubbing**.

A queen and knight in a dubbing ceremony.

The squire knelt in front of a king, queen or a lord, who tapped him on the shoulder with a sword, and said, "Arise, Sir Knight".

The life of a knight

Knights hoped their FAME as fighters would live on after their death.

Knights were meant to be CHIVALROUS – respectful and polite, especially to women.

Knights were meant to PROTECT the **Christian** religion.

War on horseback

Knights fought on horseback, riding splendid war-horses, called DESTRIERS. They were specially bred to be strong, fast and obedient. Destriers were often very fierce, kicking and biting their knight's enemies.

A good war-horse was very expensive. It cost as much as a new car does today. Rich knights took two horses with them to battle, in case one was killed or injured.

Knights used teams of **pack-horses** to carry bags of weapons and armour, and cart horses to pull wagons laden with loot, won in battle.

Riding a war-horse

Knights **STEERED** their horses using leather reins attached to a bit (a metal bar inside the horse's mouth).

Only very wealthy knights could afford armour for their horses.

METAL SPURS were fixed to the heels of a knight's shoes. He pressed them against the horse's side to make it run faster!

Weapons and armour

Knights used long swords with very sharp edges for slashing at their enemies, and short, pointed swords for stabbing them through their armour! They also carried daggers – **FOR SLITTING ENEMY THROATS.**

Knights hit out at their enemies with **maces**, **war-hammers** and battle-axes. They fended off enemy blows with wood and metal shields.

A knight on horseback carrying a mace.

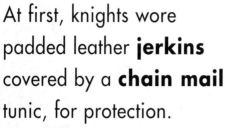

Swords from Medieval times.

At first, knights wore padded leather **jerkins** covered by a **chain mail** tunic, for protection.

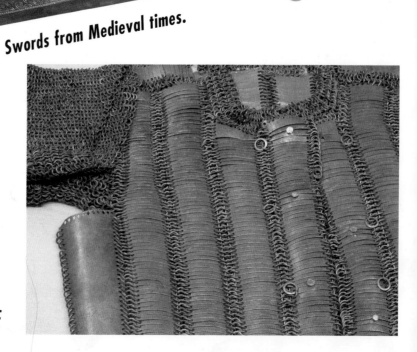

A chain mail tunic

After AD 1300, knights began to wear full-body plate-armour made of shaped metal pieces. A full suit weighed about 20 kilos, and was very hot to wear!

A suit of armour from the early 1500s.

Knights displayed **coats of arms** (family badges) on their shield or armour to help identify themselves.

In the **middle ages**, records like this were kept, showing each noble family's coat of arms.

Medieval artefacts

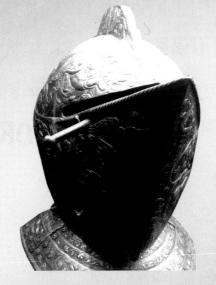

Knights wore protective HELMETS. They looked out through a moveable section called a vizor.

Knights wore metal gloves called GAUNTLETS to guard their hands.

Charge!

At the start of a battle, knights on horseback stood side by side, in rows, facing the enemy. Then, suddenly, they **CHARGED** forward at top speed, bellowing fierce war cries.

This is a medieval battle scene from the **Bayeux tapestry**, a huge piece of medieval embroidery.

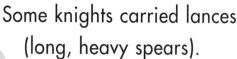

The Bayeux tapestry

Some knights carried lances (long, heavy spears). Lances could be used to knock an enemy off his horse. A knight on the ground was easier to attack. He might also get trampled by the horses!

A knight fights with a lance and sword in a battle scene from a film.

Ordinary soldiers fought on foot. They used **pikes** to stab at knights, and shot at them with long-bows and cross-bows.

Long-bowmen shoot at a knight.

A skilled long-bowman could shoot ten arrows every minute, and hit targets 300 metres away.

Medieval artefacts

LONG-BOWS were made of yew tree wood. The arrows had metal tips.

Cross-bows fired metal bolts that **SMASHED** through armour.

This metal spike is called a **CALTROP**. They were scattered in front of knights' horses, to stab their hooves and make them fall.

11

Fighting for fun

In peacetime, knights fought PRETEND BATTLES with blunt weapons. These competitions were called **jousts** and **tournaments**. They helped knights practise their skills. Kings, queens, **lords** and ladies all came to watch.

In a joust, two knights charged towards each other on horseback. The aim of the joust was to knock your opponent to the ground, using a wooden lance.

During pretend battles, knights wore surcoats (robes) over their armour. They decorated them with their family **coat of arms**.

Modern-day actors re-enact a medieval jousting competition.

Knights who lost a competition had to give their horses and armour to the winners. Some knights, who were good at fighting, became very rich this way!

Medieval artefacts

Ladies gave **LOVE-TOKENS**, such as flowers, to their favourite fighters.

Knights topped their helmets with amazing crests shaped like birds or monsters.

Knights and spectators sheltered in colourful tents at jousts.

The first castles

Castles were the biggest, STRONGEST BUILDINGS around in the **middle ages**. They were safe forts, where soldiers sheltered from enemies in wartime. Castles were also splendid homes for rich and powerful kings, **lords** and knights.

The first castles were built around AD 900. They were wooden towers called **keeps**. After AD 1050, castle-builders heaped up earth to make steep hills, called **mottes**, and built wooden keeps on top.

In later times, keeps were built in stone.

A strong, wooden fence was built around the motte. The area inside the fence was called a **bailey**. Soldiers in the castle used the bailey for keeping their war-horses safe, and for storing food supplies.

You can see a motte and bailey castle in this section from the Bayeux tapestry.

This stone keep at York replaced the original wooden one.

Early fortifications

From around 800 BC to AD 200, the Celts built tall stone towers in Scotland, called BROCHS.

Early castles and forts were built using simple tools and lots of MUSCLE-POWER. There were no power-tools or big machines!

Towers and dungeons

After AD 1000, castles were built in stone. They had **MASSIVE** stone **keeps**, surrounded by high stone walls.

Castle walls were a metre thick – or more. They were made of earth and stone rubble, pounded together, and covered with strong stone blocks on either side.

Rocks were dropped on enemies from holes called *machicolations*.

Narrow slits for shooting arrows.

This is Beaumaris Castle in Wales.

Castles were surrounded by a **moat**, a deep water-filled ditch. It could only be crossed by a drawbridge, which could be pulled up.

Castles were often used as prisons. Some had damp, underground dungeons, beneath the keep floor.

Medieval castles

This picture shows a portcullis. It could be dropped quickly to stop **ENEMIES** entering the main castle door.

The keep

Stone walls topped by battlements and walkways.

Small towers made the walls stronger. They were used as look-out posts.

Narrow, spiral, stone staircases inside towers, made it difficult for **ATTACKERS** to use their swords.

Under attack!

Enemies tried to capture castles in lots of different ways. Sometimes they dug holes under castle walls, to make them fall down. Often they CRASHED into the castle gates with **battering rams**.

Attacking armies also besieged (surrounded) castles. They camped close by and blocked off all the roads. They poisoned wells and streams, and stopped all fresh food and drink reaching the people inside.

Some attackers hurled dead bodies over the castle walls, to terrorize the people inside and spread disease.

People trapped inside a castle under **siege** had two choices – surrender and probably be killed, or starve and die!

Castle defenders fought back, throwing stones and spears. One trick was to drop red hot sand onto the attackers' heads.

Medieval warfare

This picture shows a trebuchet. It was used to SHOOT ROCKS over castle walls.

Defenders SHOT ARROWS at their attackers.

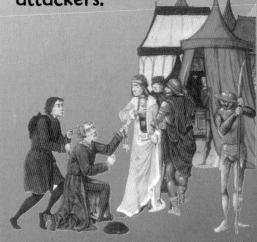

If a castle was captured, the **captain of the guard** had to hand over the keys.

Castle fun

When not at war, kings, **lords**, knights and their families liked to have fun. They invited friends and important visitors to their castles, and entertained them with FEASTS, MUSIC AND DANCING.

Lords, knights and noble ladies rode out to meadows with tame hawks (hunting birds). The hawks were trained to catch rabbits and small birds, then bring them back to their handlers.

A medieval painting of ladies on horseback.

A hawk

Knights loved to go hunting for deer and wild boar in the woods. They hunted on horseback with fierce hunting dogs.

Statues in a beautiful castle garden.

Many castles had gardens, with fountains, fruit-trees and flowers. Noble ladies liked to spend time there, listening to **minstrels** singing love songs and reciting poetry.

Castle life

In the **middle ages**, people ate with their FINGERS, spoons and knives. Forks were not normally used.

Jesters or FOOLS made everyone laugh at feasts.

CHESS became very popular in the early middle ages. This knight chess piece is over 850 years old.

Knights and castles today

From around AD **1400**, castles came **UNDER ATTACK** from new weapons called cannon. These massive tubes were filled with gunpowder. They fired huge stone cannonballs, which had the power to smash down castle walls.

In 1460, King James II of Scotland was killed when his own new cannon exploded. He was showing his wife how it worked, at the **siege** of Roxburgh Castle.

A cannon with cannon balls.

By the end of the **middle ages**, kings, **lords** and knights wanted stylish, comfortable houses to live in, and many castles fell into ruin.

Warwick castle

Today, millions of tourists visit castle ruins across Europe every year.

Often, visitors to castles can watch exciting displays where actors re-enact battles between medieval knights.

Castle myths

Since the middle ages ended, many myths have grown up about castles.

Some people believe they have seen GHOSTS in spooky castle corridors like this!

Fairy stories, such as SLEEPING BEAUTY, have been inspired by ruined castles in France.

23

Glossary

BAILEY Courtyard, surrounded by a wooden fence, outside a castle on a motte (mound).

BATTERING RAMS Huge, heavy tree trunks, used to smash castle walls and gates.

BAYEUX TAPESTRY An embroidered wall-hanging. It is about 70 metres long and shows the Norman (French) Conquest of England in 1066.

CAPTAIN OF THE GUARD The officer in charge of soldiers guarding a castle.

CELTS People who were powerful in Europe from around 800 BC to AD 200.

CHAIN MAIL Armour made of thousands of small metal rings, linked together.

CHRISTIAN RELIGION The faith of people who worship Jesus Christ.

COATS OF ARMS Special designs shown on shields, flags, badges and armour. They were a sign of high rank (your position and importance in society).

DUBBING Being tapped on the shoulders with a sword. This meant you had become a knight.

JERKINS Jackets without collars or sleeves.

JOUSTS Pretend fights between two knights.

KEEPS The strong central towers of castles.

LORDS High-ranking men who owned land. They had to be loyal to kings. Knights and ordinary people had to be loyal to lords.

MACES Spiked metal balls on sticks. They were used as weapons.

MIDDLE AGES (or medieval period) The years from around AD 500 to 1500.

MINSTRELS People who sing and play musical instruments as a job.

MOAT A very deep ditch surrounding a castle. It was often filled with water.

MOTTES Steep mounds made of earth. Keeps were built on top.

PACK-HORSES Horses used for carrying heavy loads.

PAGES Young boys learning how to be squires. They worked as messengers for knights.

PIKES Deadly weapons – sharp spikes on long poles.

SIEGE An attack on a castle (or walled city). Enemies surrounded the castle. Then they tried to break through the walls, or waited for the people inside to starve.

SQUIRES Teenage boys training to become knights. They learned fighting skills and how to ride.

TOURNAMENTS Pretend battles between teams of knights.

WAR-HAMMERS Heavy hammers, made of metal. They were used as weapons.

Index